FAITH
IS A JOURNEY

Pope Francis

FAITH
IS A JOURNEY

Meditations for
Pilgrims and Wayfarers

NEW CITY PRESS

Published in the United States by New City Press
136 Madison Avenue, Floors 5 & 6, PMB #4290
New York, NY 10016
www.newcitypress.com

Pope Francis
Faith Is a Journey – Meditations for Pilgrims and Wayfarers

First published as *La fede è un viaggio:
Meditazioni per pellegrini e viandanti*

© 2024 Dicastero per la Comunicazione
Libreria Editrice Vaticana
00120 Città del Vaticano
www.libreriaeditricevaticana.va
www.vatican.va

Cover Photo: © Xantana | Dreamstime.com

Library of Congress Control Number: 2024945524

ISBN: 978-1-56548-654-6 (paper)
ISBN: 978-1-56548-655-3 (e-book)

Vatican translations used with permission
Chapter titles are by the editor

Content

Introduction

When I was a priest in Buenos Aires (and I continued this habit as a bishop in my hometown), I loved walking through the various neighborhoods to visit fellow priests, visit a religious community, or talk to friends. Walking is good for you: It puts us in touch with what is happening around us; it makes us discover sounds, smells, and noises in the reality that surrounds us; in brief, it brings us closer to the lives of others.

To walk means to not stand still: To believe means having within us a restlessness that leads us toward a "more," toward a step forward, toward a height to reach today, knowing that tomorrow the road will take us higher—or deeper—in our relationship with God, which is exactly like the relationship with the beloveds of our life, or between friends: never finished, never taken for granted, never fulfilled, always searching, not yet satisfying. It is impossible to say with God: "Done; everything is fine; it is enough."

For this reason, the Jubilee of 2025, together with the essential dimension of hope, must push us to an ever-greater awareness of the fact that faith is a pilgrimage and that we on this Earth are pilgrims, not tourists or wanderers: We do not move randomly, existentially speaking. We are pilgrims. The pilgrim lives their journey under the banner of three keywords: risk, effort, and destination.

The risk. Today we struggle to understand what it meant for Christians of earlier times to complete a pilgrimage, accustomed as we are to the speed and comfort of our travels by plane or by train. But, to go on the road a thousand years ago meant to take the risk of never returning home due to the many dangers that could be encountered on the various routes. The faith of those who chose to set out on the journey was stronger than any fear. The pilgrims of years ago teach us to trust in the God who called them to set out toward the tomb of the Apostles, the Holy Land, or a sanctuary. We, too, ask the Lord for a small portion of that faith, to accept the risk of abandoning ourselves to his will, knowing that it is the will of a good Father who only desires for his children what is appropriate for them.

The effort. To walk effectively means to put in effort. The many pilgrims who today have returned to crowd the ancient pilgrimage routes know this well. I think of the journey to Santiago de Compostela, the Via Francigena, the various paths that arose in Italy that recall some of the most famous saints or witnesses (Saint Francis, Saint Thomas, but also Don Tonino Bello) thanks to a positive synergy between public institutions and religious bodies. Walking involves the effort of getting up early, preparing a backpack with essentials, and eating something frugal. And then there are one's feet that hurt and the thirst that becomes pungent, especially on sunny summer days. But this effort is rewarded by the many gifts that the walker encounters along the way: the beauty of creation, the sweetness of art, and the hospitality of the people. Those who make a pilgrimage on foot—many can testify to this—receive much more than the effort made. They establish beautiful bonds with people they meet on their itinerary; they experience moments of authentic silence and fruitful interiority that the frenetic life of our time often makes impossible; they understand the value of the essential compared to the glitter of having all the superfluous.

The destination. To walk like a pilgrim means that we have a landing place, that our movement has a direction, a goal. To walk means to have a destination and to not be at the mercy of chance. Those who walk have a direction; they do not wander aimlessly; they do not waste time zigzagging from one place to another. This is why I have often recalled the similarities between walking and believing: Those who have God in their hearts have received the gift of a North Star to strive for—the love we have received from God is the reason for the love we must offer to other people.

God is our goal, but we cannot reach him as we reach a sanctuary or a basilica. In fact, anyone who has made a pilgrimage on foot, finally reaching their desired destination—I am thinking of the Cathedral of Chartres, which has long been the object of a renaissance in terms of pilgrimages thanks to the initiative, which dates back a century, of the poet Charles Péguy—knows well that this does not mean to feel fulfilled. Rather, if outwardly we know well that we have arrived, inwardly we are aware that the journey is not over, because God is just like that—a milestone that pushes us further, a goal that constantly calls us to continue—because God is always greater than the idea we have of him. God himself explained it to us through the prophet Isaiah: "As the heavens are higher than the earth, so are my ways higher than your ways, and my thoughts than your thoughts" (Is 55:9). We have never arrived with God; we have never arrived at God. We are always on the move; we are always searching for him. But precisely this walking toward God offers us the inebriating certainty that he is waiting for us to give us his consolation and his grace.

Francesco

Vatican City, October 2, 2024

Editor's Note

Pope Francis often reminds us that faith "is a road to be traveled, without ever losing the goal," and this is the theme that forms the background to the meditations contained in this brief anthology. It is a collection of significant passages from the Pontiff's speeches, given on various occasions of meetings with the faithful, and is intended to offer food for thought in light of the Jubilee 2025 in particular, as its motto is "Pilgrims of Hope."

The anthology opens with a reference to the Second Vatican Council, recalling that "the Church is not a static reality, but is continually on a journey in history, toward the ultimate and wonderful goal that is the Kingdom of Heaven" (cf. p. 13). It then dwells on the daily commitment of the People of God and each believer in the search for and attainment of the common spiritual horizon, which Pope Francis affirms "means feeling called and impelled to walk together and also means disengaging from our securities and comforts in the search for a new land that the Lord wants to give us."

Believing, therefore, requires a constant, daily commitment made up of an interior search that must be accompanied by a renewed trust in one's neighbor, in order to make a common journey that leads to happiness and salvation. Those who walk, having the Lord as their traveling companion, are sure of the path they take and the goal they will reach.

Pilgrimage

Pilgrimage is of course a fundamental element of every Jubilee event. Setting out on a journey is traditionally associated with our human quest for meaning in life. A pilgrimage on foot is a great aid for rediscovering the value of silence, effort and simplicity of life. In the coming year, *pilgrims of hope* will surely travel the ancient and more modern routes in order to experience the Jubilee to the full. In Rome itself, along with the usual visits to the catacombs and the Seven Churches, other itineraries of faith will be proposed. Journeying from one country to another as if borders no longer mattered, and passing from one city to another in contemplating the beauty of creation and masterpieces of art, we learn to treasure the richness of different experiences and cultures and are inspired to lift up that beauty in prayer to God, in thanksgiving for his wondrous works. The Jubilee Churches along the pilgrimage routes and in the city of Rome can serve as oases of spirituality and places of rest on the pilgrimage of faith, where we can drink from the wellsprings of hope, above all by approaching the sacrament of Reconciliation, the essential starting point of any true journey of conversion....

In a particular way, I would like to invite the faithful of the Eastern Churches, particularly those already in full communion with the Successor of Peter, to take part in this pilgrimage. They have suffered greatly, often even unto death, for their fidelity to Christ and the Church, and so they should feel themselves especially welcome in this City of Rome that is also their Mother and cherishes so many memories of their presence. The Catholic Church, enriched by their ancient liturgies, and the theology and spirituality of their Fathers, monks and theologians, wants to give symbolic expression to its embrace of them and their Orthodox brothers and sisters, in these times when they endure their own Way of the Cross, often forced by violence and instability, to leave their homelands, their holy lands, for safer places. For them, the hope born of the knowledge that they are loved by the Church, which does not abandon them but follows them wherever they go, will make the symbolism of the Jubilee all the more powerful.

The Holy Year of 2025 is itself in continuity with preceding celebrations of grace. In the last Ordinary Jubilee, we crossed the threshold of two millennia from the birth of Jesus Christ. Then, on 13 March 2015, I proclaimed an Extraordinary Jubilee for the sake of making known and encouraging an encounter with the "merciful face of God," the core message of the Gospel for every man and woman of every time and place. Now the time has come for a new Jubilee, when once more the Holy Door will be flung open to invite everyone to an intense experience of the love of God that awakens in hearts the sure hope of salvation in Christ. The Holy Year will also guide our steps towards yet another fundamental celebration for all Christians: 2033 will mark the two thousandth anniversary of the redemption won by the passion, death and resurrection of the Lord Jesus. We are about to make a pilgrimage marked by great events, in which the grace of God precedes and accompanies his people as they press forward firm in faith, active in charity and steadfast in hope (cf. 1 Thess 1:3).

Sustained by this great tradition, and certain that the Jubilee Year will be for the entire Church a lively experience of grace and hope, I hereby decree that the Holy Door of the Basilica of Saint Peter in the Vatican will be opened on 24 December 2024, thus inaugurating the Ordinary Jubilee....

The coming Jubilee will thus be a Holy Year marked by the hope that does not fade, our hope in God. May it help us to recover the confident trust that we require, in the Church and in society, in our interpersonal relationships, in international relations, and in our task of promoting the dignity of all persons and respect for God's gift of creation. May the witness of believers be for our world a leaven of authentic hope, a harbinger of new heavens and a new earth (cf. 2 Pet 3:13), where men and women will dwell in justice and harmony, in joyful expectation of the fulfilment of the Lord's promises.

Let us even now be drawn to this hope! Through our witness, may hope spread to all those who anxiously seek it. May the way we live our lives say to them in so many words: "Hope in the Lord! Hold firm, take heart and hope in the Lord!" (Ps 27:14). May the power of hope fill our days, as we await with confidence the coming of the Lord Jesus Christ, to whom be praise and glory, now and forever.

The Pilgrim Church
to the Kingdom

In presenting the Church to the men and women
of our time, the Second Vatican Council kept in
mind a fundamental truth, one we should never forget: the Church is not a static reality, inert, an end in
herself, but is on a continual journey through history,
toward that ultimate and marvelous end that is the
Kingdom of Heaven, of which the Church on earth
is the seed and the beginning.[1] When we turn to this
horizon, we discover that our imagination falls short,
hardly able to intuit the splendor of a mystery that
surpasses our senses. And several questions spontane-
ously arise in us: When will that final step happen?
What will the new dimension that the Church enters
be like? What will become of humanity then? And of
Creation around us? But these questions are not new;
the disciples had already asked Jesus about them at
that time: "When will this come to pass? When will
the Spirit triumph over creation, over creatures, over

---

1. Cf. Dogmatic Constitution on the Church *Lumen Gentium*, n. 5.

everything...." These are human questions, time-old questions. And we, too, are asking these questions.

The Conciliar Constitution *Gaudium et Spes*, faced with these questions that forever resonate in the hearts of men and women, states, "We do not know the time for the consummation of the earth and of humanity, nor do we know how all things will be transformed. As deformed by sin, the shape of this world will pass away; but we are taught that God is preparing a new dwelling place and a new earth where justice will abide, and whose blessedness will answer and surpass all the longings for peace which spring up in the human heart" (n. 39). This is the Church's destination: It is, as the Bible says, the "new Jerusalem"—Paradise. More than a place, it is a state of soul in which our deepest hopes are fulfilled in superabundance and our being, as creatures and as children of God, reach their full maturity. We will finally be clothed in the joy, peace, and love of God, completely, without any limit, and we will come face to face with him! (cf. 1 Cor 13:12). It is beautiful to think of this, to think of heaven. We will all be there together. It is beautiful, it gives strength to the soul.

In this perspective, it is good to grasp the kind of continuity and deep communion there is between the Church in heaven and that which is still a pilgrim on earth. Those who already live in the sight of God can indeed sustain us and intercede for us, pray for us. On the other hand, we, too, are always invited to offer up good works, prayer, and the Eucharist itself, in order to alleviate the tribulation of souls still awaiting never-ending beatitude. Yes, because in the Christian perspective, the distinction is not between who is dead and who is not, but between who is in Christ and who is not! This is the point of determination, what is truly decisive for our salvation and for our happiness.

At the same time, Sacred Scripture teaches us that the fulfillment of this marvelous plan cannot but involve everything that surrounds us and comes from the heart and mind of God. The Apostle Paul says it explicitly when he says, "Creation itself will be set free from its bondage to decay and obtain the glorious liberty of the children of God" (Rom 8:21). Other texts utilize the image of a "new heaven" and a "new earth" (cf. 2 Pet 3:13; Rev 21:1), in the sense that the whole universe will be renewed and will be freed once and for all from every trace of evil and from death itself. What lies ahead is the fulfillment of a transformation that, in reality, is already happening, beginning with the death and resurrection of Christ. Hence, it is the new creation; it is not, therefore, the annihilation of the cosmos and of everything around us, but the bringing of all things into the fullness of being, of truth, and of beauty. This is the design that God, the Father, Son, and Holy Spirit, willed from eternity to realize and is realizing.

Dear friends, when we think of this magnificent reality awaiting us, we become aware of how marvelous a gift it is to belong to the Church which bears in writing the highest of vocations! So, let us ask the Virgin Mary, Mother of the Church, to keep constant watch over our journey and to help us to be, as she is, a joyful sign of trust and hope among our brothers and sisters.

Jesus, Fellow Traveler

Very often we have heard that Christianity is not merely a doctrine, or a way of behaving, or a culture. Yes, it is all this, but it is, first and foremost, an encounter. A person is Christian because he or she has encountered Jesus Christ and has let him or herself be encountered by him.

This passage of the Gospel of Luke tells us about an encounter, so as to enable us to know better how the Lord acts and how we act. We are born with a seed of restlessness. God wants it thus: the restlessness of finding fullness, the restlessness of finding God, very often without knowing that we have this restlessness. Our heart is restless; our heart is thirsty—thirsty for the encounter with God. Our heart seeks him, many times on the wrong path: it gets lost, then it returns, and it seeks him.... On the other hand, God thirsts for the encounter to the point that he sent Jesus to meet us, to come toward this restlessness.

How does Jesus act? In this passage of the Gospel (cf. Lk 24:13-35), we see clearly that he respects our situation; he does not go ahead—only at times, with the headstrong—think of Paul, when he is thrown down from the horse. But usually, he goes slowly, respecting our pace. He is the Lord of patience. How much patience the Lord has with us, with each one of us!

The Lord walks beside us, as we have seen here with these two disciples. He listens to their and our restlessness; he understands it, and at a certain point he says something to us. The Lord likes to hear us speak, to understand us well, and to give the right response to that disquiet. The Lord does not speed up his pace; he always keeps in step with us, who very often move slowly; but his patience is thus.

There is an ancient pilgrim rule that says that the true pilgrim should go at the pace of the person who is moving most slowly. And Jesus is capable of this; he does it; he does not speed up; he waits for us to take the first step. And when it is the right moment, he asks the question. In this case it is clear: "What are you discussing?" (cf. Lk 24:17). He makes himself appear ignorant so that we might speak. He is pleased when we speak to him, so that he can listen to us. And then he answers, he explains, as much as necessary. Here he says to us, "Was it not necessary that the Messiah should suffer these things and enter into His glory?" Then "beginning with Moses and all the prophets, he interpreted to them what referred to him in all the scriptures" (Lk 24:26-27). He explains, he clarifies. I confess that I am curious to know how Jesus explained, so that I may do the same. It was a beautiful catechesis.

And then the same Jesus who has accompanied us, who has drawn close to us, pretends to go on further, to see the extent of our restlessness. "Stay with us, for it is nearly evening and the day is almost over" (Lk 24:29). And in this way, we meet. But the encounter is not just at the moment of breaking bread, but it's in the entire journey. We meet Jesus in the darkness of our doubts, even in the ugly doubt of our sins; he is there to help us, in our anxieties. He is always with us.

The Lord accompanies us because he wants to meet us. That is why we say that the core of Christianity is an encounter: it is the encounter with Jesus. "Why are you a Christian?" Some, because of tradition. Others cannot say why, because they met Jesus, but they did not realize it was an encounter with Jesus. Jesus is always looking for us. Always. And we have our restlessness. In the moment in which our restlessness meets Jesus, that is where the life of grace begins, life in its fullness, the life of the Christian journey.

May the Lord give us all this grace to meet Jesus every day, to know, to be aware that it is really he who is walking with us in all the moments of our lives. He is our pilgrim companion.

Walk According to the Spirit

In the passage from the Letter to the Galatians that we have just heard, Saint Paul exhorts Christians to *walk according to the Holy Spirit* (cf. Gal 5:16, 25); there is a style: *to walk according to the Holy Spirit*. In effect, to believe in Jesus means to follow him, to follow him along his way, just as the first disciples did. At the same time, it means avoiding the opposite way, that of selfishness and of seeking one's own interests, which the Apostle calls the "desires of the flesh" (v. 16). The Spirit is the guide for this journey along the way of Christ, a wonderful but also difficult journey that begins in Baptism and lasts our entire lives. Let us think of it as a long excursion to the mountain heights: it is breathtaking, and the destination is attractive, but it requires a lot of effort and tenacity.

This image can be helpful to understand the merit of the Apostle's words: "to walk by the Spirit," "to be led" by the Spirit. They are expressions that indicate an action, a movement, a dynamism that prevents us from stopping at the first difficulties but elicits confidence in the power "coming from above."[2] Walking along

---

2. *Shepherd of Hermas* 43, 21.

this path, the Christian acquires a positive vision of life. This does not mean that the evil present in the world disappears, or that the negative impulses of our selfishness and pride diminish. Rather, it means that belief in God is always stronger than our resistance and greater than our sins. And this is important!

As he exhorts the Galatians to follow this path, the Apostle places himself on their level. He abandons the verb in the imperative—"walk" (v. 16)—and uses the indicative "we": "let us walk also by the Spirit" (v. 25). That is to say, let us walk along the same line and let us be led by the Holy Spirit. It is an exhortation. Saint Paul feels this exhortation is necessary for himself as well. Even though he knows that Christ lives in him (cf. 2:20), he is also convinced that he has not yet reached the goal, the top of the mountain (cf. Phil 3:12). The Apostle does not place himself above his community. He does not say, "I am the leader; you are those others; I have reached the top of the mountain, and you are [still] on the way." Rather, he places himself in the midst of everyone's journey in order to provide a concrete example of how necessary it is to obey God, corresponding ever more and ever better to the Spirit's guidance. And how beautiful it is when we find pastors who journey with their people, who do not separate themselves from them. This is very beautiful. It is good for the soul.

This walking by the Spirit is not only an individual task: it also concerns the community as a whole. In fact, building up the community according to the way indicated by the Apostle is exciting but demanding. The desires of the flesh that we all have, that is, the temptations, jealousies, prejudices, hypocrisies, and resentments, continue to make themselves felt. Having recourse to a rigid set of precepts can be an easy temptation. But doing this would mean straying from the path of freedom, and instead of climbing to the top, it would mean returning to the bottom. Journeying along the way of the Spirit requires, first of all, giving space to grace and charity, making space for God's grace, and not being afraid.

After speaking sternly to them, Paul invites the Galatians to bear each other's difficulties, and should someone make a mistake, to use gentleness (cf. 5:22). Let us listen to his words: "Brethren, if a man is overtaken in any trespass, you who are spiritual should restore him in a spirit of gentleness. Look to yourself, lest you too be tempted. Bear one another's burdens, and so fulfill the law of Christ" (6:1-2). This is an attitude that is quite different from gossiping, which is not according to the Spirit. What is according to the Spirit is being gentle with a brother or sister when correcting him or her, and keeping watch over ourselves with humility so as not to fall into those sins.

In effect, when we are tempted to judge others badly, as often happens, we must first reflect on our own weaknesses. How easy it is to criticize others! But there are people who seem to have a degree in gossip. They criticize others every day. Take a look at yourself! It is good to ask ourselves what drives us to correct a brother or a sister, and if we are not in some way co-responsible for their mistake. In addition to giving us the gift of gentleness, the Holy Spirit invites us to be in solidarity, to bear others' burdens. How many burdens there are in a person's life: illness, lack of work, loneliness, pain! And how many other trials that require the proximity and love of our brothers and sisters! Saint Augustine's words commenting on this same passage can also help us: "Therefore, brothers, if a man has been caught out in some wrongdoing ... correct him in a spirit of gentleness. And if you raise your voice, love within. If you encourage, if you present yourself as a father, if you reprove, if you are severe, love."[3] Love always. The supreme rule regarding fraternal correction is love and to want the good of our brothers and sisters. It is a matter of tolerating the problems of others and the defects of others in the silence of prayer, so as to find the right way to help them to correct themselves. And this is not easy. The

---

3. Cf. Sermon 163/B 3.

easiest path is to gossip. Talking behind someone else's back as if I am perfect. And this should not be done. Gentleness. Patience. Prayer. Proximity.

Let us walk with joy and patience along this path, allowing ourselves to be led by the Holy Spirit.

On the Way

(from *L'Osservatore Romano*)

For Christians, Jesus is the way, and the journey of life is part cross and part resurrection. But on the way there are those who freeze like "spiritual mummies," who are stubborn and go astray, who spend their life spinning their wheels, mesmerized by worldly beauty. During Mass at Santa Marta, the Pope warned against these attitudes and expressly invited an examination of conscience in order to verify our personal experience of faith.

The day's passage from the Gospel of John (14:5-14), Francis explained, "is part of Jesus' lengthy discourse at the Last Supper, his farewell speech; he is bidding farewell before going to his passion." Jesus tells the Apostles, "I will not leave you orphans; I will not leave you alone; I will go to prepare a place for you." Moreover, the Pope pointed out, in the "two verses before this passage that we have listened to," we read, "You know the way where I am going," and Thomas responds, "Lord, we do not know where you are going; how can we know the way?" This is where the day's passage begins, with Jesus saying to Thomas,

"I am the way." This is "the response to the anguish, the sorrow, the sadness of the disciples over Jesus' farewell; they do not understand very well, and thus they are sad." This is why Jesus says to Thomas, "I am the way."

Jesus' expression, Francis said, "makes us think about Christian life," which "is a journey; with Baptism, we begin to walk and walk and walk." One might say that Christian life "is a journey, and the correct way is Jesus." Thus, Jesus said precisely, "I am the way." Therefore, "in order to walk correctly in Christian life, Jesus is the way."

But, the Pope warned, "There are many ways to journey." There is "first of all that of not walking. A Christian who doesn't walk, who doesn't make his way, is an 'un-Christian' Christian, so to speak; he is a somewhat pagan Christian, standing there, standing still, immobile. He does not go forward in Christian life. He does not bring the Beatitudes to fruition in his life. He does not do works of mercy. He stands still." Moreover, Francis added, "Pardon the word, but it is as if he were a mummy—a spiritual mummy." Indeed, "there are Christians who are spiritual mummies," standing still, "they don't do anything bad, but they don't do anything good." However, this way of being "does not bear fruit; they are not fruitful Christians because they do not walk."

Then, the Pope continued, there are some who "walk and go astray," as "we too, often go astray." It is "the Lord himself who comes and helps us. It is not a tragedy to go astray." In fact, "the tragedy is being stubborn and saying, 'This is the way,' and not letting the Lord's voice tell us, 'This is not the way, turn around and go the right way'." It is important to go back to the right path "when we realize our errors, the mistakes we make" and "not to be stubborn and always go astray, because this distances us from Jesus, because he is the way."

Yet, Francis explained, "There are others who walk but don't know where they are going: they are misguided in Christian life, wanderers." Their life amounts to "roaming, here and there, thus losing the beauty of drawing near to Jesus in life." In short, "they lose their way because they roam and so often this roaming," this "misguided wandering, leads them to a life with no way out: too much wandering transforms life into a labyrinth, and then they don't know how to get out." Thus, in the end, "they have missed Jesus' call, they have no compass to find the way out, and they wander, they roam, they search."

Then, the Pope continued, "there are others on the journey who are seduced by beauty, by something, and they stop midway, mesmerized by what they see, by that idea, by that proposal, by that landscape, and they stop." But "Christian life is not a charm; it is truth. It is Jesus Christ." And "Teresa of Avila said, speaking about this journey, 'We are walking in order to arrive at the encounter with Jesus'." In other words, just "as a person walking to get somewhere doesn't stop because he likes a hotel, because he likes the landscape, but he goes onward, onward, onward." However, "in Christian life" it is okay "to pause, to look at the things I like, things of beauty—there are beautiful things, and we must look at them, because God made them—but without stopping." Indeed, "Christian life must continue." It is important to ensure "that something beautiful, something peaceful, a peaceful life does not mesmerize me so as to stop me." Thus, the Pope affirmed, there are "many ways not to take the right path," because "the righteous journey, the right way is Jesus."

In this regard, the Pontiff recommended an examination of conscience through a series of direct questions. "We can ask ourselves today, each one of us, the following: How is my Christian journey, which I began in Baptism? Am I standing still? Have I gone astray? Am I constantly wandering, not knowing where to go spiritually? Do I stop at things that I like: worldliness, vanity—so many things, no?—or do I always go forward, making the Beatitudes and the works of mercy tangible?" And, he added, "it is good to ask ourselves this: it is a true examination of conscience!" Essentially, "How am I walking? Am I following Jesus?"

The Pope explained that in the First Reading, Paul told us "how to follow Jesus": "I delivered to you what I also received, that Christ died for our sins in accordance with the Scriptures, that he was buried, that he was raised on the third day in accordance with the Scriptures, and that he appeared to Cephas, then to the twelve." But "this is life" and "when Jesus tells Thomas, 'I am the way,' he is telling him this." Therefore, the Pontiff continued, "this is the journey, and it is the Christian path: the way of Jesus is so full of comfort, of glory, also of the cross, but always with peace in the heart."

Drawing his reflection to a close, the Pope reaffirmed that "by not completely following Jesus, that Christian is standing still. One who has gone astray, one who is mesmerized and seduced by beauty or by things that interest him, stops there to look and delays the journey."

Before returning to the celebration, Francis again called for an examination of conscience—at least five short minutes—to ask ourselves these questions: "How am I doing on this Christian journey? Standing still, gone astray, wandering around, stopping at the things I like?" Or do I correspond to what Jesus says: "I am the way"? And, Pope Francis said, "Let us ask the Holy

Spirit to teach us to walk correctly, always, and when we get tired" let us take a short rest and go on. "Let us ask the Lord for this grace."

So Many Reasons to Run

Dear young people,

I thank you also because this appointment has been preceded by an interweaving of so many paths on which you have made yourselves pilgrims, together with your bishops and priests, traveling along the roads and paths of Italy, in the midst of the treasures of culture and faith that your fathers have bequeathed. You have traveled through the places where people live and work, rich in vitality and marked by toil, in cities as well as in villages and remote hamlets. I hope you have breathed deeply the joys and difficulties, the life and faith of the Italian people.

In the Gospel passage we heard (cf. Jn 20:1-8), John tells us about that unimaginable morning that changed human history forever. Let's imagine that morning: At first light on the day after the Sabbath, around Jesus' tomb, everyone starts running. Mary of Magdala runs to warn the disciples; Peter and John run to the tomb. Everyone is running; everyone feels the urgency to move. There is no time to lose; we must hurry, as Mary had done—remember?—as soon as she conceived Jesus, to go and help Elizabeth.

We have many reasons to rush, often just because there are so many things to do and there is never enough time. Sometimes, we rush because something new, something beautiful, something interesting attracts us. Sometimes, on the contrary, we run to get away from a threat, a danger. Jesus' disciples run because they have received the news that Jesus' body has disappeared from the tomb. The hearts of Mary of Magdala, Simon Peter, and John are filled with love and beat wildly after the parting that seemed final. Perhaps the hope of seeing the Lord's face again is rekindled in them! As on that first day when he promised, "Come and see" (Jn 1:39). The one who runs the hardest is John, certainly, because he is younger, but also because he did not stop hoping after seeing with his own eyes Jesus die on the cross, and also because he was close to Mary, and because of that he was "infected" by her faith. When we feel that faith is failing or is lukewarm, we go to her, Mary, and she will teach us, understand us, and make us feel faith.

Since that morning, dear young people, history has not been the same. That morning changed history. The hour when death seemed to triumph actually turned out to be the hour of its defeat. Not even that heavy boulder, placed before the tomb, could stand. And from that dawn of the first day after the Sabbath, every place where life is oppressed, every space where violence, war, and misery dominate, there where man is humiliated and trampled upon, in that place a hope of life can still be rekindled.

Dear friends, you have set out and come to this meeting. And now my joy is to hear that your hearts beat with love for Jesus, like those of Mary Magdalene, Peter, and John. And because you are young, I, like Peter, am happy to see you running faster, like John, driven by the impulse of your heart, sensitive to the voice of the Spirit that animates your dreams. That is why I say to you, do not be content with the cautious pace of those who line up at the back of the line. It requires courage to take a leap forward, a bold and daring leap to dream and realize, like Jesus, the Kingdom of God, and to commit yourselves to a more fraternal humanity. We need fraternity: take risks, go ahead!

I will be happy to see you running stronger than those in the Church who are a little slow and fearful, attracted by that Face so loved, whom we adore in the holy Eucharist and recognize in the flesh of our suffering brother. May the Holy Spirit impel you in this forward rush. The Church needs your momentum, your insights, and your faith. And when you reach where we have not yet reached, have the patience to wait for us, as John waited for Peter before the empty tomb.

Shrines and Popular Spirituality

Going on pilgrimages to shrines is one of the most eloquent expressions of the faith of the People of God and manifests the piety of generations of people who, with simplicity, have believed in and entrusted themselves to the intercession of the Virgin Mary and the saints. This popular religiosity is a genuine form of evangelization that needs to be always promoted and valued, without minimizing its importance. It is curious: Blessed Paul VI, in *Evangelii nuntiandi*, speaks of "popular religiosity" but says it is better to call it "popular piety," and then, the Latin American Episcopate in the Aparecida Document goes a step further and speaks of "popular spirituality."

All three concepts are valid when taken together. In the shrines, in fact, our people live their deep spirituality, that piety that for centuries has shaped the faith with simple but very meaningful devotions. Let us think of how intense, in some of these places, is the prayer to Christ crucified, or that of the Rosary, or the Stations of the Cross.

It would be a mistake to assume that those who go on pilgrimage live a spirituality that is not personal but "mass." In reality, the pilgrim brings with him his own story, his own faith, the lights and shadows of his life. Everyone carries in his heart a special desire and a special prayer. Those who enter the shrine immediately feel that they are at home, welcomed, understood, and supported.

I really like the biblical figure of Anna, the mother of the prophet Samuel. She, in the temple at Silo, with her heart swollen with sadness, prayed to the Lord to have a son. The priest, Eli, on the other hand, thought she was drunk and wanted to kick her out (cf. 1 Sam 1:12-14). Anna well represents many people we may meet in our shrines. Eyes fixed on the crucifix or the image of Our Lady, a prayer made with tears in her eyes, filled with trust. The shrine is truly a privileged space to meet the Lord and to touch his mercy. To confess in a shrine is to experience touching God's mercy firsthand.

This is why the keyword I would like to emphasize with you today is welcome—welcoming pilgrims. With welcoming, so to speak, we stake everything on it. A loving, festive, cordial, and patient welcome. It also takes patience! The Gospels present us with Jesus who is always welcoming to those who approach him, especially the sick, the sinners, and the outcasts. And we remember that expression of his, "he who welcomes you welcomes me, and he who welcomes me welcomes him who sent me" (Mt 10:40).

Jesus spoke of welcome, but more importantly, he practiced it. When we are told that sinners—for example, Matthew, or Zacchaeus—welcomed Jesus into their home and to their table, it is because, first and foremost, they had felt welcomed by Jesus, and this had changed their lives. It is interesting that the Book of the Acts of the Apostles ends with the scene of St. Paul who, here in Rome, "welcomed all who came to him" (Acts 28:30). His house, where he lived as a prisoner, was the place where he proclaimed the Gospel. Welcoming is really crucial for evangelization. Sometimes, simply a word, a smile, is enough to make a person feel welcomed and appreciated.

The pilgrim who arrives at the shrine is often tired, hungry, and thirsty. And many times, this physical condition also mirrors the inner one. Therefore, this person needs to be welcomed well on both the material and spiritual levels. It is important that the pilgrim who crosses the threshold of the shrine feels treated not so much like a guest but as a family member. He or she must feel at home, expected, loved, and looked upon with eyes of mercy. Whoever they may be, young or old, rich or poor, sick and afflicted or a curious tourist, may they find the welcome they are due because in everyone there is a heart that seeks God, sometimes without fully realizing it.

Let every pilgrim have the joy of finally feeling understood and loved. In this way, upon returning home, they will feel nostalgia for what they have experienced and will want to go back, but most of all, they will want to continue the journey of faith in their ordinary life.

A very special welcome is the one offered by God's ministers of forgiveness. The shrine is the house of forgiveness, where everyone encounters the tenderness of the Father who has mercy on everyone, no one excluded. Those who approach the confessional do so because they are repentant of their sin. They feel the need to approach there. They clearly perceive that God does not condemn them, but welcomes them and embraces them, like the father of the prodigal son, to restore his filial dignity (cf. Lk 15:20-24). Priests ministering in shrines must have their hearts imbued with mercy; their attitude must be that of a father.

Walking Together

To go on pilgrimage is to realize that we are, in a way, returning home as a people and to realize, too, that we are a people. A people whose wealth is seen in its myriad faces, its myriad cultures, languages, and traditions—the holy and faithful People of God who, in union with Mary, advance on their pilgrim way singing of the Lord's mercy. In Cana of Galilee, Mary interceded with Jesus to perform his first miracle; in every shrine, she watches over us and intercedes, not only with her Son but also with each of us, asking that we not let ourselves be robbed of fraternal love by those voices and hurts that provoke division and fragmentation. Complicated and sorrow-filled situations from the past must not be forgotten or denied, yet neither must they be an obstacle or an excuse standing in the way of our desire to live together as brothers and sisters.

To go on pilgrimage is to feel called and compelled to journey together, asking the Lord for the grace to change past and present resentments and mistrust into new opportunities for fellowship. It means leaving behind our security and comfort and setting out for a new land that the Lord wants to give us. To go on pilgrimage means daring to discover and communicate the mystique of living together, and not being afraid to mingle, to embrace, and to support one another. To go on pilgrimage is to participate in that somewhat chaotic sea of people that can give us a genuine experience of fraternity, to be part of a caravan that can together, in solidarity, create history (cf. *Evangelii Gaudium*, 87).

To go on pilgrimage is to look not so much at what might have been (and wasn't), but at everything that awaits us and cannot be put off much longer. It is to believe in the Lord who is coming and even now is in our midst, inspiring and generating solidarity, fraternity, and the desire for goodness, truth, and justice (cf. *Evangelii Gaudium*, 71). To go on pilgrimage is to commit ourselves to ensuring that the stragglers of yesterday can become the protagonists of tomorrow and that today's protagonists do not become tomorrow's stragglers. And this, dear brothers and sisters, requires a certain skill, the art of weaving the threads of the future. That is why we are here today, to say together, *Mother, teach us to weave the future!*

As pilgrims to this shrine, we turn our gaze to Mary and to the mystery of God's election. By saying "yes" to the message of the angel, Mary—a young woman from Nazareth, a small town in Galilee on the fringes of the Roman Empire and of Israel itself—set in motion the revolution of tenderness (cf. *Evangelii*

Gaudium, 88). Such is the mystery of God's election: He looks to the lowly and confounds the powerful; he encourages and inspires us to say "yes," like Mary, and to set out on the paths of reconciliation.

Brothers and sisters, let us not forget that the Lord does not disappoint those who take a risk. Let us journey, then, and journey together. Let us take a risk and allow the Gospel to be the leaven that permeates everything and fills our peoples with the joy of salvation, in unity and in fraternity.

Not To Be Existential Tourists

(From *L'Osservatore Romano*)

The Pontiff spoke about the value trusting in the Lord has in a Christian's life since the Lord "never disappoints." Pope Francis emphasized that "The First Reading contains God's promise, that which awaits us, that which God has prepared for us: 'Behold, I create new heavens and a new earth ... the former things shall not be remembered,' the struggles ... all will be new. I create Jerusalem for joy. There shall be joy." It is the promise of joy.

Before God asks anything of us, he always makes a promise, the Bishop of Rome explained. Therefore, the fundamental principle of the virtue of hope is confidence in the Lord's promises. "This hope," he affirmed, "does not disappoint, for he is faithful and does not disappoint." The Lord, he continued, has never told anyone to go, to act, without first making him a promise. "Even Adam, when he was driven out of Paradise, departed with a promise." This, he said, "is our destiny, to walk with a view to the promises, confident that they will become a reality. It is beautiful to read chapter 11 of the Letter to the Hebrews, where the journey of the People of God toward the promises is recounted. This people so loved the promises, they sought them even to the point of martyrdom. They knew that God was faithful. Hope never disappoints."

To further explain the value of trusting in the Father's promises, the Pope cited the day's passage from the Gospel of John (4:43-54), which recounts the episode of the king's official. Upon learning that Jesus had arrived in Cana, the official went and begged him to come and save his son who was ill and at the point of death. The Pope observed that it was enough for Jesus to say, "Go; your son will live," for the official to believe and set off on his journey home. "This is our life: to believe and take to the road" like Abram, who "trusted in the Lord and also journeyed amid hardship and difficulty." For example, Abram's faith "was put to the test" when he was asked to sacrifice his son Isaac. "He journeyed. He trusted in the Lord, and he set out. This is the Christian life—journeying toward the promises." That is why "the Christian life is hope," the Pope said.

Yet we can also fail to journey in life, the Pope remarked. "In fact, there are many Christians and Catholics who do not journey. There is a temptation to come to a standstill. Some feel they are good Christians because they belong to Church movements. Many Christians have come to a standstill.... Their hope is weak. Yes, they believe that heaven exists, but they are not seeking it. They follow the Commandments, and they fulfill all the precepts, all of them, but they have come to a standstill. The Lord does not find in them a leaven to help his people grow, and this is a problem—people at a standstill" in their spiritual lives.

"Then there are others," he added, "who have taken the wrong road. All of us, at times, have taken the wrong path." Of course, the Pope continued, "we all sometimes take the wrong turn. The problem is not taking the wrong road; the problem is not turning back once we realize that we have made a mistake. The fact that we are sinners is what causes us to choose the wrong path. We can return: the Lord gives us the grace to be able to return."

Finally, "there is another, even more dangerous group because they deceive themselves," the Pope said. They "journey but make no headway. There are wandering Christians: they go round and round as though life were an existential tour with no goal and end ... they do not take the promises seriously. They go round and round and deceive themselves for they say, 'I am walking....' No; you are not walking, you are wandering! The Lord asks us not to stop, not to take the wrong road and not to wander through life. He asks us to look to the promises, to go forward with the promises before us," like the man from the Gospel of John, who "believed in Jesus' promises and took to the road." It is faith which enables us to set out and continue on the journey.

Lent, Pope Francis concluded, is a propitious time to consider whether we are on the journey or instead "have come to a standstill." If so, we must repent. Or if we "have taken the wrong road," then we must go to confession in order "to set out on the right path once more," or lastly, we are "theological tourists," like those who wander through life but never advance. "Let us ask the Lord for the grace," Pope Francis urged, "to get back on the road, to set out on the journey toward the promises. As we consider this, it will benefit us greatly to reread chapter 11 of the Letter to the Hebrews "for a correct understanding of what it means to walk toward the promises which the Lord has made."

Fellow Travelers of Youth

Your Association is turning seventy. This is a good milestone, but it is only part of a journey. Indeed, to make the most of the precious journey you have taken so far, you are called to grow further, to develop your activities, and to spread many other good fruits. Just seventy years ago, some young people from the Catholic Action Youth, traveling with Don Carlo Carretto on the train that took them to Geneva, had the idea of founding the Youth Tourism Center. They felt this truly as an inspiration, so much so that after less than two months, they established the Association, under the leadership of Don Carlo, proposing to become bearers, through multiple recreational and cultural activities, of social ties inspired by participation and an integral vision of the human person, cultivating the dream of inspiring and transforming the social environment.

Speaking of an "integral vision of the person," we certainly do not mean a theory, but a way of living and acting; this vision is not found first of all in a manual, but in people who live in this style: with their eyes open to the world, with their hands holding other hands, with their hearts sensitive to the weaknesses of their brothers and sisters. We could also say that the "wholeness" to which you refer does not allude to perfection, but to imperfection; it does not recall the completeness of the individual, but rather his incompleteness and the need to look around to understand each other more deeply; it does not lead to a proud immobilization of the self, but rather to the humble search for ever new knowledge, of contact with people, cultures, and the issues of our time.

It is with these goals that your Association promotes tourism, tourism not inspired by the canons of consumerism or eagerness only to accumulate experiences, but tourism that favors the encounter between people and the territory, and one that fosters understanding and mutual respect. If I visit a city, it is important that I not only know the monuments but also that I realize what history it has behind it, how its citizens live, and what challenges they try to face. If I climb a mountain, besides keeping myself within the limits that nature imposes on me, I will have to respect it, admire its beauty, and protect its environment, and thus create a bond with the natural elements made up of knowledge, recognition, and appreciation.

You have wisely defined this way of traveling as "slow tourism," as opposed to mass tourism, as it promotes quality and experience, solidarity, and sustainability. You have chosen a tortoise as a mascot of this careful and constructive tourism, depicted on this year's membership card, which with its determined calm, teaches us that slowness—if it is not the result of laziness—generates attention to places and people, loyalty to the earth, and dedication to it.

Now, the practice of slow tourism, based on cultural and environmental considerations and education, helps you to experience every moment of everyday life, including those of work and other important commitments, in a different and more conscious way. I, therefore, hope you will be able to maintain the breadth of your horizons, to experience spaces with the watchful slowness of the tortoise, and to inspire leisure time in a joyful and free way.

As I greeted you, I made reference to the typical enthusiasm of your age; however, we must acknowledge that many young people, instead of wishing to build the future, unfortunately, feel disillusioned and unmotivated. Perhaps because of the pessimism that surrounds them, they do not dare to fly high but are content to survive or to run. This is bad when a young person just gets by and does not truly live, as if he has already "retired," and it is bad for a young person to be retired! Precisely in the light of your spirituality, within the Youth Tourist Center, you can become travel companions for many of your peers; you can help them bring back enthusiasm if they no longer perceive it because they are buried by the rubble of disenchantment or by the dust of bad examples. Sharing free time as quality time can become a good key to opening the door of the hearts of many young people, generating bonds of friendship capable of conveying authentic values and faith itself.

Sources

Pilgrimage
Spes non Confundit, Bull of Indiction of the
Ordinary Jubilee of the Year 2025.

The Pilgrim Church to the Kingdom
General Audience, St. Peter's Square,
Wednesday, November 26, 2014.

Jesus, Fellow Traveler
Homily in the Chapel of Casa Santa Marta,
Sunday, April 26, 2020.

Walk According to the Spirit
General Audience, Paul VI Audience Hall,
Wednesday, November 3, 2021.

On the Way
Morning Meditation in the Chapel of Casa Santa Marta,
Tuesday, May 3, 2016 (*L'Osservatore Romano*, Weekly ed.
in English, n. 19, May 13, 2016).

So Many Reasons to Run
Final Reflection at the Prayer Vigil with Italian Youth,
Rome, Circo Massimo, August 11, 2018.

Shrines and Popular Spirituality

Jubilee of Pilgrimage Workers and Shrine Rectors,
Paul VI Hall, January 21, 2016.

Walking Together

Homily, Shrine of Sumuleu-Ciuc, Saturday, June 1, 2019.

Not To Be Existential Tourists

Morning Meditation in the Chapel of Casa Santa Marta,
Monday, March 31, 2014 (*L'Osservatore Romano*,
Weekly ed. in English, n. 14, April 4, 2014).

Fellow Travelers of Youth

Address to the Directors and Associates of the Youth Tourist
Center, Paul VI Audience Hall, Friday, March 22, 2019.

FOCOLARE MEDIA
Enkindling the Spirit of Unity

The New City Press book you are holding in your hands is one of the many resources produced by Focolare Media, which is a ministry of the Focolare Movement in North America. The Focolare is a worldwide community of people who feel called to bring about the realization of Jesus' prayer: "That all may be one" (see John 17:21).

Focolare Media wants to be your primary resource for connecting with people, ideas, and practices that build unity. Our mission is to provide content that empowers people to grow spiritually, improve relationships, engage in dialogue, and foster collaboration within the Church and throughout society.

Visit www.focolaremedia.com to learn more about all of New City Press's books, our award-winning magazine *Living City*, videos, podcasts, events, and free resources.

NEW CITY PRESS